SERVICE
LEARNING

Volunteering
to Help in Your
Neighborhood

Claudia Isler

HIGH
interest

books

Children's Press
A Division of Grolier Publishing
New York / London / Hong Kong / Sydney
Danbury, Connecticut

For Eric, who welcomed me into his neighborhood

Photo Credits: Cover, p. 8, 13, 14, 17, 18, 25, 26, 29, 30, 36 © Indexstock imagery; p. 4 © Paul A. Sanders/Corbis; p.7 © Reuters Newmedia Inc/Corbis; p. 11 © Kelly-Mooney Photography/Corbis; p.21 © Morton Beebe, S.F./Corbis; p.33 © Julie Habel/Corbis; p.35 Illustration by Michael DeLisio; p. 41 © R.W. Jones/Corbis

Contributing Editors: Rob Kirkpatrick and Mark Beyer
Book Design: Michael DeLisio

Visit Children's Press on the Internet at:
http://publishing.grolier.com

Library of Congress Cataloging-in-Publication Data

Isler, Claudia.
    Volunteering to help in your neighborhood / by Claudia Isler.
       p. cm. – (Service learning)
    Includes bibliographical references and index.
    ISBN 0-516-23374-2 (lib. bdg.) – ISBN 0-516-23574-5 (pbk.)
    1. Voluntarism—Juvenile literature. 2. Social action—Juvenile literature.
       3. Young volunteers—Juvenile literature. [1. Voluntarism. 2. Social
       action.] I. Title. II. Series.

HN49.V64 I75 2000
361.3'7—dc21
                                                                            00-027381

CONTENTS

INTRODUCTION

Everyone's neighborhood is a community. Communities are made up of people who live together, work together, and help one another. You are a member of a community whether you live in a big city or a small town, in an apartment building or on a farm.

People who live in communities have always helped each other. Long ago, people hunted together for food to feed their communities. More recently, governments and schools have helped to launch important service organizations.

In 1961, President John F. Kennedy set up the Peace Corps. This organization sends volunteers (unpaid workers) all over the world to help people in need. In 1964, President Lyndon B. Johnson began an organization called VISTA (Volunteers in Service to America), as well as other groups: the

People like to live in a safe and happy neighborhood.

National Teacher Corps, the Job Corps, and University Year of Action.

In 1990, President George Bush created the Points of Light Foundation. This organization gives all Americans the opportunity to volunteer their time to help others. When Bill Clinton was elected, he established AmeriCorps and the Corporation for National Service. These groups create even more opportunities for Americans to help their communities.

You don't have to join one of these national organizations to help out. Today, people help their neighborhoods in many ways. They have food drives to collect canned goods for hungry families. They volunteer to clean up trash from sidewalks. They help recycle to reduce waste. They visit sick children or the elderly in hospitals. These activities make volunteers active members of their communities. These opportunities also teach students useful skills and important lessons that they can use later in life.

President Clinton addresses AmeriCorps volunteers.

CHAPTER ONE

WHAT IS SERVICE LEARNING?

Service-learning projects are run by volunteers. These volunteers give their time and skills to work on a project that helps others. A teacher or adviser guides the project. He or she meets with you before and during the project to see how it is progressing. You also meet with your adviser after the project to discuss what you learned. This process of self-evaluation is an important part of service learning.

HOW SERVICE LEARNING HELPS YOU

The real payoff of a service-learning project is what you learn about yourself and other people. You'll get a sense of how your

Students and teachers join efforts in starting a service program.

actions affect the community in which you live.

Service learning can have other benefits, too. Many schools give academic credit for participation in service-learning projects. Some organizations give certificates and scholarships to service learners. Service-learning work can build your self-confidence. You also can develop skills for the future.

HOW SERVICE LEARNING HELPS OTHERS

Neighborhoods survive best if the people who live in them help one another. Poor people may need help getting food for their families. Students who have trouble in school may need to be taught how to read or do simple math. Sick or elderly people may just need someone to visit them or read to them. No matter where you live, there are people who could use your help.

Working with the elderly is one way that you can help your neighborhood.

NEIGHBORHOOD NEEDS

The kind of help your community needs depends on the kind of neighborhood in which you live. Some neighborhoods have abandoned buildings or dirty streets. These neighborhoods would be much nicer places to live if the trash was cleaned up and flowers planted. Some neighborhoods have a high crime rate. Young people have created programs to "take back the streets." They patrol the area in groups with adults and report any suspicious people or activities to the police. Does your community have a recycling program? If not, maybe you can help to start one. If you improve the place where you live, you make life better for everybody else who lives there.

FUN FACT

In October 1999, "The Oprah Winfrey Show" featured kids who volunteered to help their communities. President Bill Clinton called in to the show to offer his support.

Your neighborhood may benefit from a recycling program.

CHAPTER TWO

GETTING STARTED

Does service-learning work sound like something you'd like to do? How can you get started? It's easier than you think. As you read this book, more than five million secondary-school students are involved in a service-learning program or project. Now, you can be one of them!

SERVICE-LEARNING PROGRAMS AT SCHOOL

Many schools have service-learning programs. Often, students who participate in service-learning projects get school credits. Check with your teacher or guidance counselor to see if your school has a service-learning program.

Teachers can help you get started in service learning.

Campus Contact

Campus Contact is an organization which arranges federally-sponsored programs in communities throughout the country. Each year, students volunteer more than 22 million hours to Campus Contact programs.

PROGRAMS OUTSIDE OF SCHOOL

Schools are not the only places that have service-learning programs. Several national organizations, such as AmeriCorps, sponsor programs in which students can help improve their neighborhood. Businesses in your area also may give money to groups that work on community-related projects.

AmeriCorps

AmeriCorps is like a Peace Corps in which students volunteer in the United States. AmeriCorps gives thousands of students across the country the chance to spend a year serving their communities. For example, in

Volunteers can patrol your neighborhood and help to keep it safe.

Buffalo, New York, AmeriCorps "rangers" patrolled high-crime areas. They helped bring down crime by 48 percent. In return for volunteer work, AmeriCorps awards money to student volunteers to help pay for college.

PICKING THE RIGHT PROJECT FOR YOU

Once you find a service-learning program, pick the right kind of activity for you. Start by figuring out how much time you can give to a project. How much time do you need for homework, extracurricular (outside of class)

This AmeriCorps service learner is teaching how to give CPR.

work, and household chores? Can you volunteer only a couple of hours per week? Can you work after school, or only on the weekends? Some people can give more time than others. That's okay. Just make sure you don't commit to something that requires more time than you can give. That will only make more work for the rest of the group.

You also should find a service-learning project that interests you. Do you hate getting wet? Then don't sign up to work on a fund-raising car wash. Do you enjoy drawing or painting? You may want to help make posters for your service-learning project. The best service-learning volunteer is one who enjoys his or her project.

NEIGHBORHOOD SAFETY

You might volunteer for service-learning programs that help to make your neighborhood a safer place. You might help as a crossing guard on streets that are dangerous to cross. You might teach kids to wear helmets when they ride bikes. You might organize first aid and CPR classes. You might fix broken street lamps, or clear traffic signs that are blocked by overgrown trees and bushes. You also can organize a service-learning group to fix safety problems in your neighborhood.

SERVICE-LEARNING PROGRAM SAVES FAMILY!

by Eliza Berkowitz

PITTSBURGH—Firefighters in Pittsburgh work together with service-learning students. They teach local residents what to do in case of an emergency. Their work was lifesaving for a six-year-old girl and her family. She saved her family from a fire in their house by dialing 911. She'd been taught to dial 911 by a student volunteer.

KEEPING YOUR NEIGHBORHOOD HEALTHY

One way to keep your neighborhood healthy is to make sure that everyone has enough to eat. Food banks and co-ops work with service learners to organize food drives. They help get affordable food to low-income families.

Another way to help people in your community is to teach them about the

If your neighborhood has homeless people, your service-learning group could help them find food and shelter.

dangers of smoking. Your group could plan a neighborhood "smoke out," when smokers promise to give up smoking for that day.

Do a lot of people in your community suffer from the cold during the winter? A service-learning group could collect winter coats and warm blankets for the poor. Every year in New York City, volunteers give thousands of coats to homeless people.

Habitat for Humanity

In many communities, some people have no homes. They are forced to live on the street. To help fight homelessness, some communities work with Habitat for Humanity. Habitat for Humanity is a volunteer organization that builds homes for needy families.

Keeping Kids away from Cigarettes

Thirteen-year-old Deanna Durrett wanted to see how easy it was for underage kids to buy cigarettes. She went throughout her hometown and found twenty machines where she could buy a pack of cigarettes. She told her story to state officials. Her work helped Kentucky politicians pass a law that states cigarette machines must be supervised by store managers. Deanna was named the 1999 National Youth Advocate of the Year for the Campaign for Tobacco-Free Kids.

KEEPING YOUR NEIGHBORHOOD CLEAN

Your service-learning group could fight pollution in your neighborhood. Pick an area. It can be your street, school grounds, or the local park. Then, start cleaning it up! Create eye-catching posters that remind people not to throw trash on the street. Begin a recycling program. Organize a group to paint over graffiti. Ask the city government to pass laws for harsher fines for littering. Work to get trash cans placed on corners where lots of people leave things in the street. Organize a tree-planting effort. Beautify an area with flowers. You can do many things to make your community a cleaner place.

Beautify Your Block

In New York City, a seventeen-year-old student organized an event she called Beautify Your Block. She convinced local business owners to donate all the supplies she needed. She taught residents how to plant and care for their window flower boxes. The street looked better when the event was done, and residents got the chance to meet, talk, and have fun.

A HAPPY NEIGHBORHOOD

Your neighborhood will be a better place if its residents are happy. Are there older people in your neighborhood who could use some help around the house? Is there a retirement home in your neighborhood? Many older people feel lonely. They would enjoy the company of young people. Volunteers could talk to them or read to them. Maybe they'd enjoy playing a game of Scrabble.

Do you like reading and children? Your group could volunteer to read to kids at the local library. You could organize a book drive to increase your library's collection.

Do you enjoy sports and teamwork? You could organize teams and events for people

Senior members of your neighborhood may enjoy meeting and talking with service learners.

living with physical and mental challenges. You could create a sports program or run activities for younger kids at the local park. You might be able to gather donations of balls, bats, jump ropes, and whatever else you need.

Fast Fact

Almost half of all community colleges in the United States have service-learning programs.

CHAPTER THREE

STARTING YOUR OWN SERVICE-LEARNING PROGRAM

What if your school or community does not offer a service-learning program? Or what if your local service-learning program does not offer an activity that interests you? You can still be involved in service-learning by starting your own program!

Starting your own program takes a lot more time and effort than joining an existing program. But all of the extra work can pay off in a big way when you finish a project that you organized!

GETTING PERMISSION

Before you get started, you'll need to find a teacher, counselor, or principal at school to

You and your friends can start your own service-learning program.

27

advise you. Explain what kind of service-learning project you want to do. Then ask him or her if he or she will help you get started. Having a school official help you with your service-learning program can be very important. He or she can get you permission to use school property or supplies. Also, your adviser might be able to arrange for you to get school credit when you have completed your project.

When you recruit other students for your service-learning project, you need to make sure that everyone is allowed to participate. Parents are concerned about their children's time and where they're spending it. They also will want to know if they have to drive the kids somewhere. Write a permission slip to explain your group's goal. Make sure to write how much time will be required of student volunteers.

Working together can be both fun and productive.

BUILDING A TEAM

You probably can find enough volunteers at school. You also can try to find volunteers at a church, temple, or community center. To get volunteers, you need to get out your message. Design posters and hang them in hallways at school. You could set up an information table in your school's cafeteria.

How about a neighborhood snow-shoveling project?

Let's say you want to create teams to shovel snow from sidewalks and driveways during the winter. Get to know your volunteers. What are their interests? What special skills do they have? One person may be great at writing. Another may be good at designing posters. Another may be good at working with people. He or she could find elderly people in your neighborhood who need their driveways shoveled. Remember: Every volunteer has something special that he or she is good at doing.

MAKE A PLAN

It's important to set goals right away. You should avoid complicated plans. Keep things simple. Once your plan is clear, write a mission statement.

Mission Statement

A mission statement is a document that states your goals. It also describes your plans for accomplishing those goals. A mission statement will come in handy when you have to explain your project to advisers or sponsors. Here's a sample:

"Shovel It! is a volunteer organization. We are committed to shoveling snow from the sidewalks and driveways of the elderly and physically disabled. We believe that our actions will make the neighborhood safer. It also will establish a relationship between students and the community. Volunteers will use their free time during the winter to seek out those who need assistance."

FINDING SPONSORS

A lot of projects require money. For example, students in "Shovel It!" might need to purchase snow shovels. They also might need money for art supplies to make posters.

There are different ways to get money for a service-learning project. The U.S. government offers grants (money set aside to fund such projects). Your teacher can help you to apply for grants. You could do some fundraising by holding bake sales or book sales. You could recycle bottles and cans, or ask for donations.

Fast Fact

In Newport News, Virginia, the mayor's office runs a program called Rent-a-Teen. Residents call Rent-a-Teen when they need someone to mow their lawn, baby-sit, or help clean out a garage, for example. The kid who does the job gets paid. This could be one way for your group to earn money.

*A car wash is a good way to raise
funds for your service-learning program.*

ADVERTISING

To get your project off the ground, you'll need
to make sure people know about it. Posters,
sign-up sheets, and fund-raising events are
good ways to advertise your service-learning
project. You can make press releases and
flyers to get out the message. Your group also
can deliver a public service announcement.

Press Release

A press release is an advertisement that is sent to television and radio stations and newspapers. It should have a brief description of your project under a catchy headline. Include a phone number or e-mail address of a contact person.

Flyers

In your flyers, describe your project. Explain when and where your events will take place. Make sure the flyer is eye-catching and easy to read.

Public Service Announcement (PSA)

A public service announcement (PSA) is a short message read on the air. Contact your local television and radio stations. They will tell you how to submit your PSA and what their guidelines are. Most PSAs are between 10 and 30 seconds long. An announcer will read your PSA for free.

Flyers such as this one can promote service-learning projects.

WHAT: Schoolwide Smoke Out!
WHEN: Friday, May 14
SPONSORED BY THE CENTRAL H.S.
SERVICE-LEARNING PROGRAM

CHAPTER FOUR

EVALUATING YOUR PROJECT

A big part of service learning involves your own thoughts on the project. Your group adviser will want to know how your project went. What worked well? What didn't work as well? What would you do differently? Most importantly, what did you learn about yourself? What did you learn about other people?

KEEPING A JOURNAL

Keeping a journal is a great way to evaluate your project. Your teacher or adviser may require you to keep a journal. Get a notebook or blank book. Use it to keep track of your activities. Write down what you did each day. Describe the people with whom you worked.

Keep a journal to remember and reflect on your service work.

Make sure you describe what worked well, what problems you had, and what you did to solve those problems. You also could take pictures of your group project and make a photo album.

Afterward, you will be able to look through your journal. Your journal will make it a lot easier to evaluate your project when you're done. Almost all of the information you'll need will be right there at your fingertips.

From Your Neighborhood to the 'Net

If you know how to use the Internet, you may want to develop a Web page. You could use your Web page to describe your service-learning program. If you know how to use a scanner, you even can put photos from your project onto your site.

MEETING NEW PEOPLE

One of the most exciting things about doing service learning in your neighborhood is the chance to meet people and make new friends. You could work with some kids you never really knew before. Working together for a common cause can form the basis for lasting friendships.

WHAT NEW EXPERIENCES DID YOU HAVE?

Did you organize and lead a team of volunteers? Was this your first time working with others toward a common goal? Were you able to get along with others? Did you come up with ways to work out problems? The skills that you developed in your service-learning project can help you later in life. Service-learning skills such as team management look impressive on college applications. When you apply for jobs, employers will be more likely to hire you. To them, your service-learning experience will show that you have had success in solving problems and meeting goals.

HAVE YOU MADE YOUR NEIGHBORHOOD BETTER?

Depending on your project, this may be a difficult question to answer. Did you plant trees and flowers? Then parts of your neighborhood may look better. The Shovel It! volunteers cleared driveways. This made it easier for elderly people to leave their homes. What if your group organized a food drive, a coat drive, or a neighborhood watch group? How did your project help people in your neighborhood?

Local History and Folklore

You could start a service-learning program to lead a research project about your town. Do you know anything about the history of your town? How old is your town? How did it get its name? Did any historic battles happen in your area? Was a president, inventor, athlete, or celebrity born there? Did any myths or folktales come from your area? The result of your research could be published in the community library. Then, the whole town can benefit from your project.

Service work can be a fun way to make your neighborhood a better place in which to live.

Once you've had time to think about the work you have done, ask yourself: Do you want to participate in service learning in the future? Would you like to do the same project again, or work on a different one? Either way, you've learned that service learning is a great way to make your neighborhood a better place to live.

NEW WORDS

advertise to announce publicly by printed or broadcasted messages

adviser someone who leads or guides group members

community an area where people live and work

co-op an organization owned by and run for the benefit of those using its services

CPR (cardiopulmonary resuscitation) procedure used to bring back a person's normal breathing after something causes the heart to stop

extracurricular any activity that is not a part of your classes, such as sports teams or clubs

flyer an eye-catching message printed on paper that is passed out to describe an event, project, or program

folktale a story or legend handed down from generation to generation

grant money awarded by the U.S. government to fund a project

neighborhood a type of community

organizational skills the abilities to make arrangements and plans to carry out a task successfully

press release a written statement that is sent to television, radio stations, and newspapers in order to promote an event or project

public service announcement (PSA) a short message read on television or radio to promote an event or project

recycle to use again; to return for future use

volunteer a person who does a job willingly, without payment

Books

Duper, Linda Leeb. *160 Ways to Help the World: Community Service for Young People.* New York: Facts on File, Inc., 1996.

Hoose, Phillip. *It's Our World, Too!: Stories of Young People Who Are Making a Difference.* Boston: Joy Street Books, 1993.

Lewis, Barbara A., and Pamela Espeland. *The Kid's Guide to Service Projects: Over 500 Service Ideas for Young People Who Want to Make a Difference.* Minneapolis, MN: Free Spirit Publishing, 1995.

Lewis, Barbara A., Pamela Espeland, and Caryn Pernu. *The Kid's Guide to Social Action: How to Solve the Social Problems You Choose— And Turn Creative Thinking into Positive Action.* Minneapolis, MN: Free Spirit Publishing, 1998.

Ryan, Bernard, Jr. *Community Service for Teens: Opportunities to Volunteer.* Chicago: Ferguson Publishing, 1998.

Corporation for National Service: Learn & Serve America!
1201 New York Avenue, NW
Washington, D.C. 20525
(202) 606-5000
Web site: *www.cns.gov/learn/index.html*
At this site, you'll learn about service-learning programs in schools and community organizations across the country. You also can find out about honors and scholarships for student volunteers.

Habitat for Humanity International
121 Habitat Street
Americus, GA 31709-3498
(912) 924-6935
Web site: *www.habitat.org*
The site provides information on how the program works and how to get involved.

National Crime Prevention Council
1000 Connecticut Avenue, NW
13th floor
Washington, D.C. 20036
(202) 466-6272
Web site: *www.ncpc.org*
The site explains what young people can do
to take action in their neighborhoods.

Youth Service America
1101 15th Street, NW, Suite 200
Washington, D.C. 20005
(202) 296-2995
Web site: *www.ysa.org*
This site is dedicated to helping kids find
worthwhile volunteer opportunities. It con-
tains valuable links to help you learn more
about volunteering and to help you find a
volunteer project.

INDEX

ABOUT THE AUTHOR

Born and raised in New York City, Claudia Isler has edited material ranging in subject from robotic engineering to soap operas. She is the author of other books for young people, including *Caught in the Middle: A Teen Guide to Custody*. She now lives with her husband in a neighborhood of deepest dark-est Pennsylvania, where she works as a writer and editor.